KIDS' ALASKA

Workbook of Alaska and its History

By: Noël Maxwell

Good Roots Press
www.goodrootspress.com

For my wonderful family -
Dave, Alyssa, Hayden, Ryan & Anna -
who thought I'd never get off the computer.

"Mom" by Alyssa

Published by:
Good Roots Press
PO Box 3493
Homer, AK 99603
Email: dave@goodrootspress.com
www.goodrootspress.com

ISBN: 0-9745187-0-0

Cover art by Molly O'Neill - one of our talented Alaskan kids!

Table of Contents

Dear Readers,

This book is for everyone who wants to learn more about our "Alyeska" or "Great Land!" Each page includes a game or activity, as well as information about Alaska's geography, peoples, or history. Whether you are just visiting Alaska or live here year-round, you are sure to learn something new. Use it to quiz your brother, sister, parent, or grandparent when you are on one of those long Alaskan car trips! If you get stuck, all the answers are in the back.

You can do it just for fun, or include it as part of an Alaskan History Curriculum. However you use it - have fun with it! Read it, draw in it, doodle on it, and learn about Alaska!

Enjoy!

Noël Maxwell
Homer, Alaska

Welcome to The Last Frontier!

It's time to explore Alaska!

See if you can locate these popular destinations by matching the small pictures below to the same ones on the map.

- Mt. McKinley - North America's Tallest Mountain
- Nome - Finish Line for the Iditarod Sled Dog Race
- Homer - "Halibut Fishing Capital of the World"
- Aleutian Chain - Chain of Islands extending 1,200 Miles
- Ketchikan - Wettest City in America (156-162 in/yr)
- Kodiak - "King Crab Capital of the World"
- Yukon Delta National Wildlife Refuge - Over 1 Million Birds Roost Here
- Glacier Bay National Park - Breathtaking Views of Calving Glaciers
- Barrow - Northernmost Town on North American Continent
- Juneau - Alaska's Capital City
- Anchorage - Alaska's Largest City
- Valdez - "Switzerland of Alaska"
- Chilket Bald Eagle Reserve – Over 3,500 Eagles Feast on Salmon
- Fairbanks - "Golden Heart of Alaska"
- Katmai National Park - "Valley of 10,000 Smokes"
- Skagway- Door to the Klondike Goldfields
- Seward - Sea Life Center / Kenai Fjords National Park
- Musk Ox Farm - Only Musk Ox Farm in the World
- Tok - "Dog Capital of Alaska"
- Kobuk Valley National Park - Largest Active Sand Dunes in the Artic (25 sq. miles)

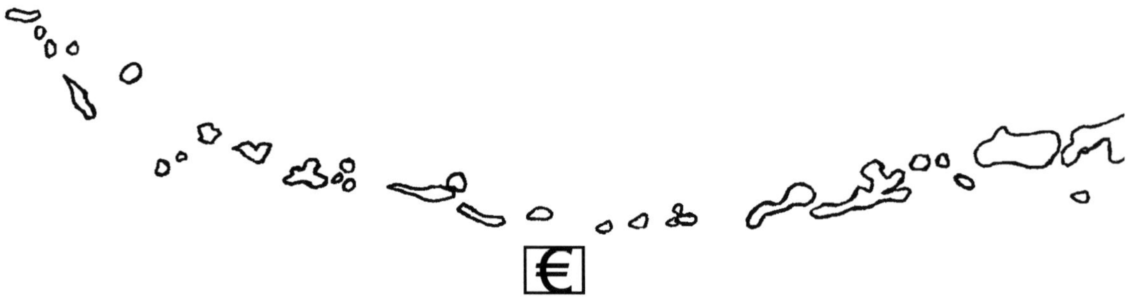

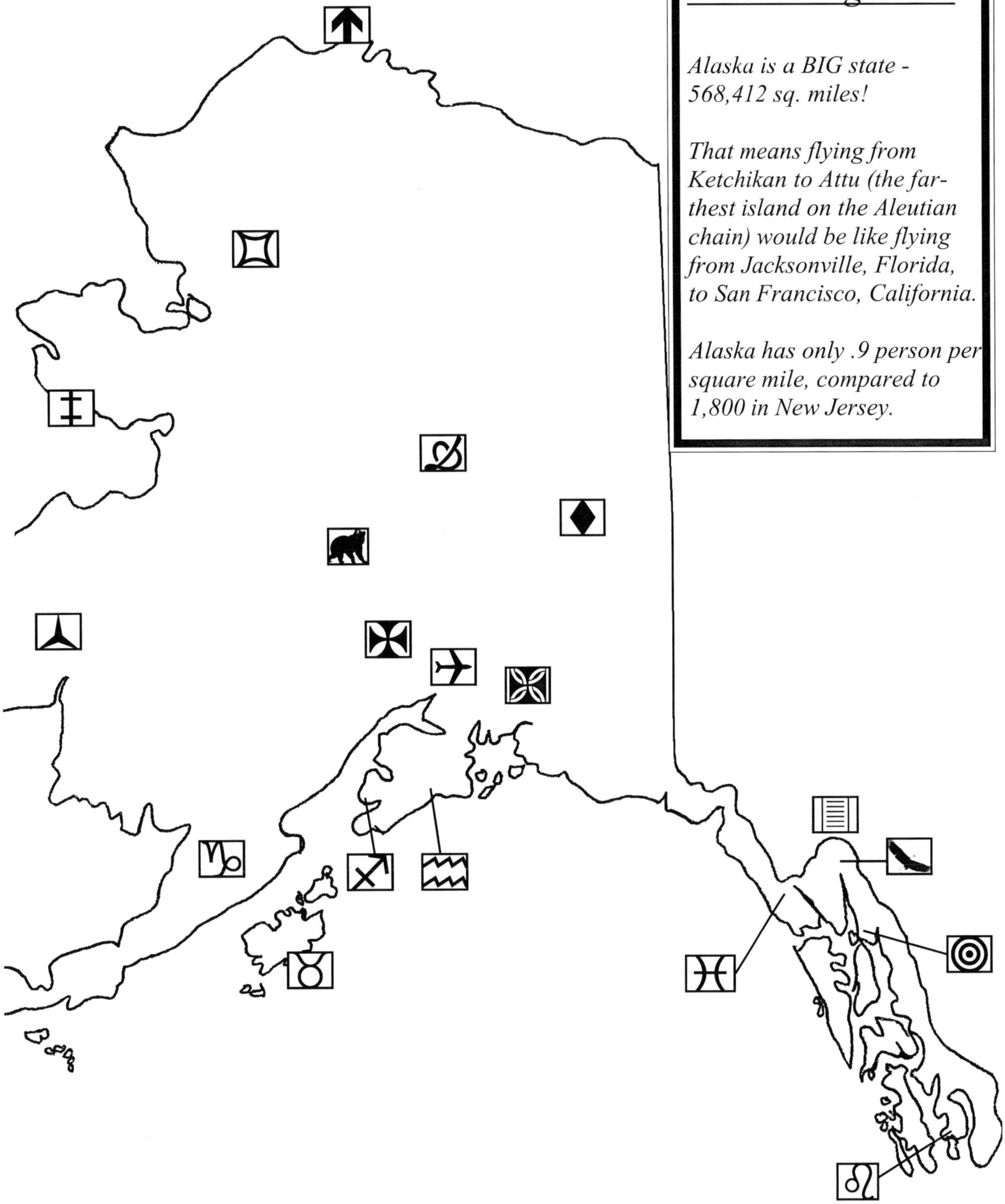

Fascinating Facts:

Alaska is a BIG state - 568,412 sq. miles!

That means flying from Ketchikan to Attu (the farthest island on the Aleutian chain) would be like flying from Jacksonville, Florida, to San Francisco, California.

Alaska has only .9 person per square mile, compared to 1,800 in New Jersey.

Alaska's Animals

Many wild animals call Alaska home. Keep your eyes open. You never know what you might see! Just a few of our special critters are pictured below. If you don't know all their names, check out the list on next page.

How many can you name? (Note: Raccoons are only found in Southeast Alaska.)

Animal Tracks

Sometimes these sneaky animals can be close by. You roll out of the sack one bright morning and find fresh tracks right outside your tent! Would you know what sniffed your head while you were asleep?

Test your knowledge by identifying the tracks below.

Mountain Goat	Wolf	Puffin	Raccoon	Musk Ox
Grizzly Bear	Eagle	Moose	Beaver	Lynx
Sandhill Crane	Red Fox	Caribou	Porcupine	Sandpiper

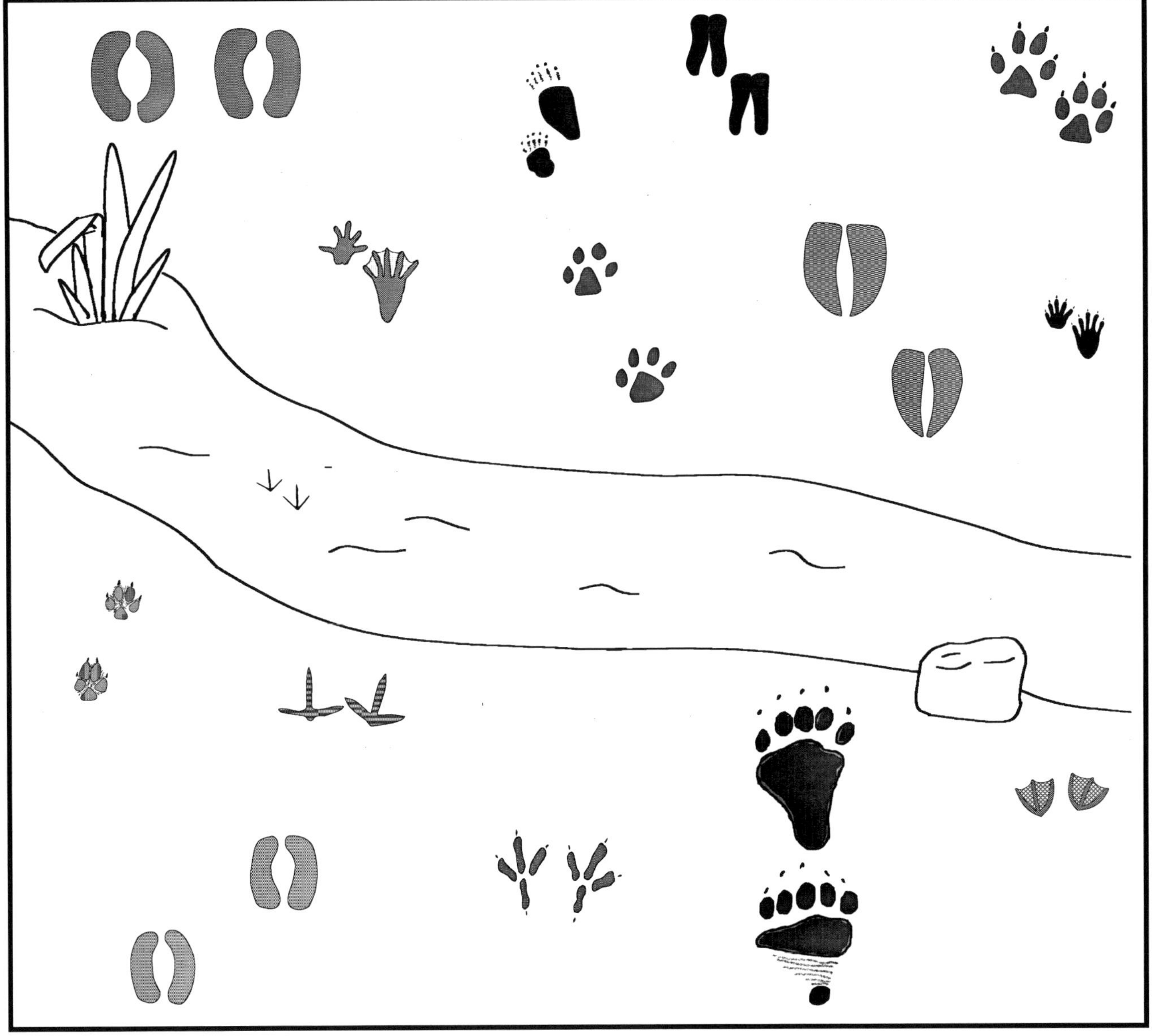

Alaska's Underwater Animals

For years explorers, traders, and tourists have come for the abundant fish and sea animals found in Alaska's seas, rivers, and lakes.

Fish for these animals in this sea of words.

salmon	starfish	octopus	halibut	skate
crab	trout	clams	snails	shrimp
whale	otter	seal	oysters	

A	M	X	N	S	O	T	T	E	R	N	Y
U	Y	Y	K	A	T	M	G	Y	V	D	G
R	J	V	T	Z	S	A	C	L	A	M	S
S	G	U	O	H	K	T	R	T	C	M	M
A	S	Z	T	C	A	A	A	F	E	I	B
L	N	O	W	H	T	L	B	H	I	A	X
M	A	Y	D	H	E	O	I	F	W	S	I
O	I	S	R	S	A	C	P	B	F	O	H
N	L	T	H	L	S	L	J	U	U	X	W
L	S	E	A	L	R	Q	E	Z	S	T	L
E	T	R	O	U	T	C	X	T	L	H	U
Q	P	S	H	R	I	M	P	E	I	L	I

State Symbols

Each state picks a variety of symbols - a state flag, song, bird, bug, flower, mineral, tree, etc. - to express its unique characteristics.

Do you know Alaska's State Symbols? If not, the next few pages should help you out.

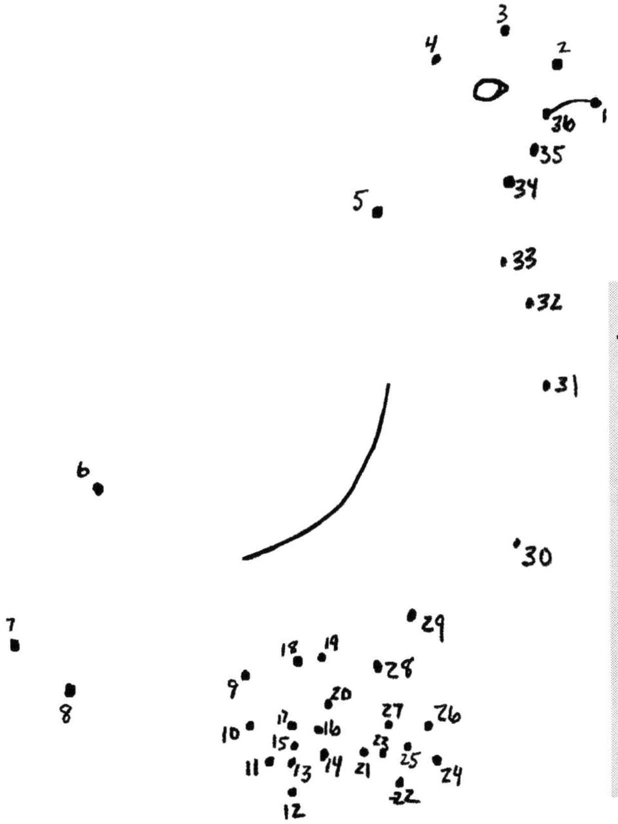

Alaska State Bird: *What am I?*

I wear white in the winter, but don a brown jacket in spring. (Use the secret code below to fill in the spaces to find out.)

___	___	___	___	___	___
23	9	12	12	15	23

___	___	___	___	___	___	___	___	___
16	20	1	18	13	9	7	1	14

Alaska State Flower: *What am I?*

My name comes from a Greek word that means "mouse ear" because of the shape of my petals.

___	___	___	___	___	___	-	___	___	-	___	___	___
6	15	18	7	5	20		13	5		14	15	20

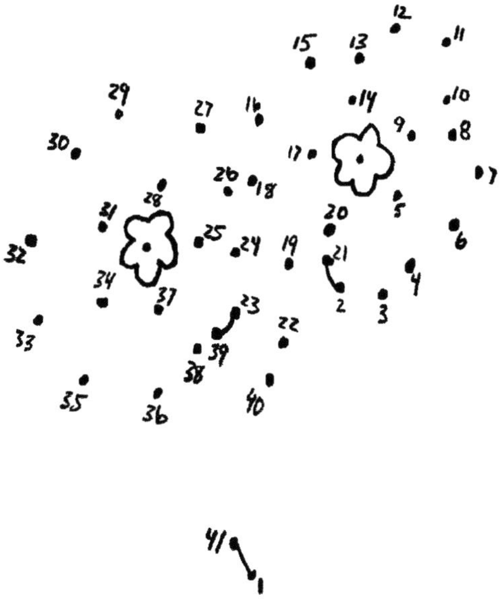

Secret Code

A	B	C	D	E	F	G	H	I	J	K	L	M	N
1	2	3	4	5	6	7	8	9	10	11	12	13	14

O	P	Q	R	S	T	U	V	W	X	Y	Z
15	16	17	18	19	20	21	22	23	24	25	26

State Flag

Alaska Territorial News 1926

ATTENTION!

All students in 7-12 grades.

Alaska Flag Contest!

Prize: $1,000

And the Winner is ...
Benny Benson!!

Out of 142 entries, Benny Benson, a 13 year old from Chignik, Alaska, submitted the winning design. Here is how he described the flag:

> The blue field is for the Alaska sky and forget-me-not, an Alaskan flower. The North Star is for the future state of Alaska, the most northerly of the Union. The dipper is for the Great Bear - symbolizing strength.

From his description, color this flag.

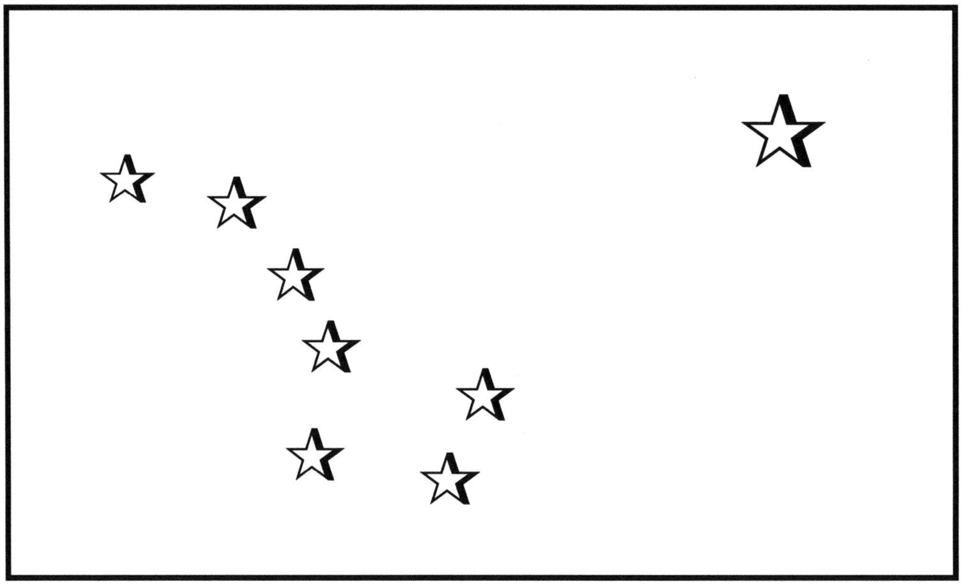

The contest for the flag was held in 1926 when the United State Congress first granted territorial status to Alaska. It became the official flag of the Territory of Alaska on May 2, 1927. When Alaska became the 49th state in 1959, Benny's flag became Alaska's State Flag.

State Song

The Alaska flag was the inspiration for the following poem written by Maria Drake, Assistant Commissioner of Education, in 1935. Later, Elinor Dusenbury set the poem to music, and it became Alaska's official state song.

Alaska's Flag

Eight stars of gold on a field of blue - Alaska's flag.
May it mean to you the blue of the sea, the evening sky,
The mountain lakes, and the flow'rs nearby;
The gold of the early sourdough's dreams,
The precious gold of the hills and streams;
The brilliant stars in the northern sky,
The "Bear" - the "Dipper" - and, shining high,
The great North Star with its steady light,
Over land and sea a beacon bright.
Alaska's flag - to Alaskans dear,
The simple flag of a last frontier.

Calling All Poets!

Poems are fun! You try writing one. Below is a list of rhyming words and an example to get you started.

After you are done, try to come up with a tune to go with it!

Rhyming Words

Bear	Gold	Moose
hair	old	loose
wear	fold	goose
Lake	**Fish**	**Sky**
bake	wish	fly
rake	dish	try

Here's ours:

Ol' Sam came for the
gold,
Tho' he sought it 'til he
was old,
He never found no
dough,
But wound up an old
Sourdough.

Now you try:

OTHER STATE SYMBOLS

Draw lines to match the clue to the right answer.

1. State Capital	Mastodon
2. State Nickname	Mount McKinley
3. State Motto	Jade
4. State Tree	King Salmon
5. State Mineral	Four-spot Skimmer Dragonfly
6. State Gem	Bowhead Whale
7. State Fish	Juneau
8. State Sport	Land of the Midnight Sun
9. State Fossil	Sitka Spruce
10. State Marine Mammal	Dog Mushing
11. State Insect	Yukon River
12. State Land Mammal	Gold
13. Highest Point	Sea Level
14. Lowest Point	North to the Future
15. Longest River	Moose

SCORE

15	OLD SOURDOUGH	5 - 10	HIBERNATING BEAR
10 - 14	SPAWNING SALMON	0 - 5	MOOSE CALF

State Seal

The State Seal represents Alaska's government and is used to make government papers official. The design includes some of the unique features of our state.

The sun design represents the northern lights. What else do you see?

Alaska Close - Up: Southeast Alaska

Welcome to the 'Pan-Handle' of Alaska! Southeast Alaska is a 560 mile long strip of land connected on one side to Canada and bordered on the other by a series of islands called the Alexander Archipelago. The huge mountains and glaciers of the Coastal Range form a natural barrier between Alaska and Canada.

Most of the Southeast is inaccessible by car, so what do you do? Ride the ferry on the Alaska Marine Highway System or fly or go on a cruise!

You're the Captain!

Guide your ship through the Inside Passage, stopping at all the Ports of Call to enjoy the breathtaking beauty and abundant wildlife!

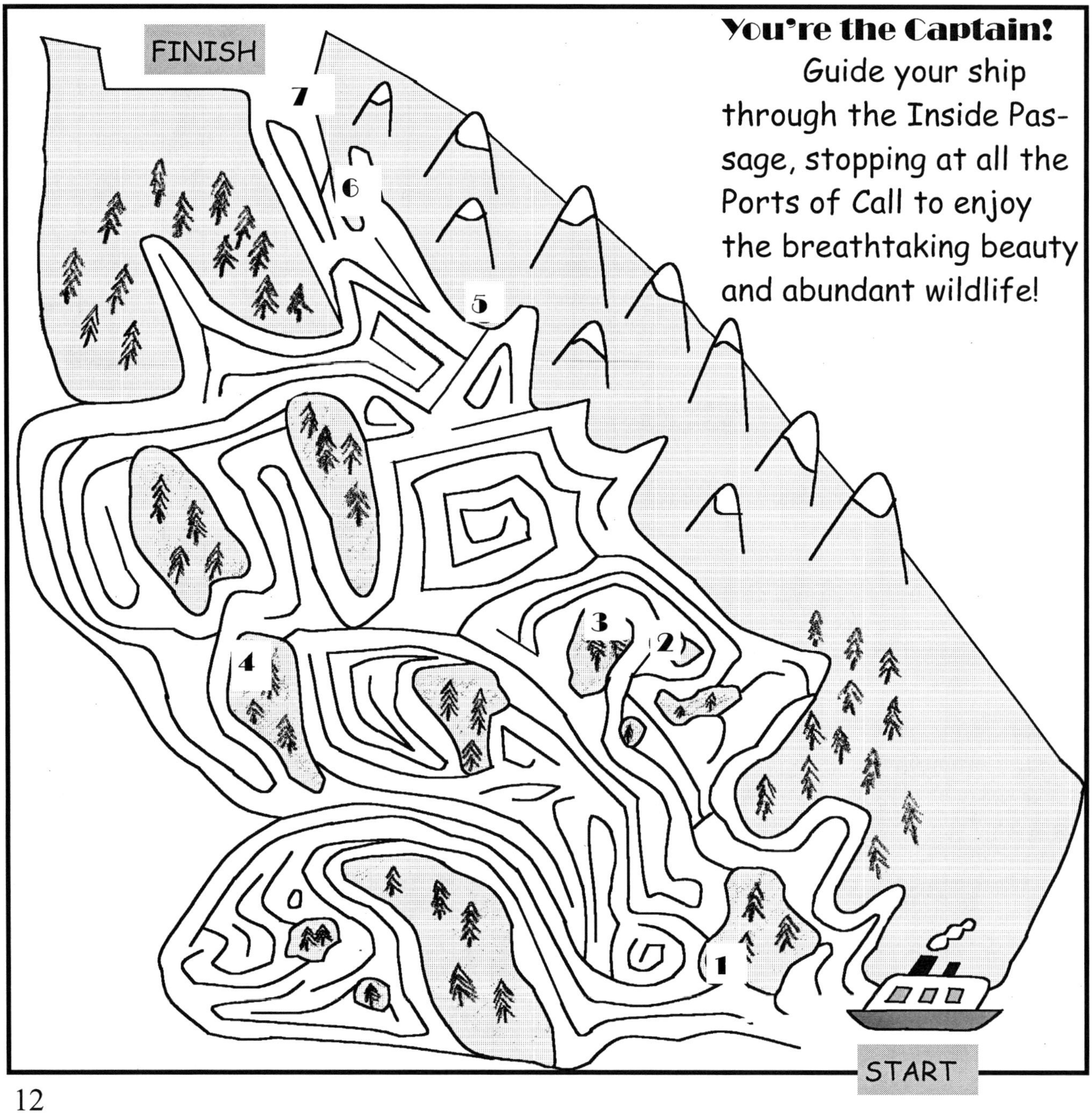

Help! Somehow the names of the towns got all mixed up. Cross out every other letter to find the names of these cities. The first letter of each word is correct.

Inside Passage: Ports of Call

1. KMESTWCPHQIVKDAZN

"Rain Capital of the World" with 156 to 162 in./yr.

Attractions:

Largest Collection of Totem Poles in the World

2. WMRYAENVGAEPLWL

Attractions:

Petroglyphs (ancient rock carvings)

Stikine (STIK-een) and Tlingit (KLINK-it) Totem Poles

3. PHERTKEXRLSMBAUPRFG

"Little Norway"

Attractions:

Humpback whales

Rosemaling - traditional Scandinavian house painting

4. SOIWTQKGA

Attractions:

Sitka National Historical Park - wildlife sanctuary & center for Indian and Russian history and art.

Saint Michael's Orthodox Cathedral

5. JCUPNSEIAPU

Alaska State Capital

Attractions:

Alaska State Museum

Saint Nicholas Russian Orthodox Church - oldest Russian Church in Alaska

6. HYABIVNEERS

Attractions:

Doorway to Chilkat Eagle Preserve

Sheldon Museum and Cultural Center

Fort William Henry Seward Historic District

7. STKJAFGDWTAKY

Attractions:

Klondike Gold Rush National Historical Park

?

Clue: Up to 4,000 eagles come to feast on the salmon in my river. I boast of one of the largest concentrations of eagles in the world.

What am I?

?

Clue: Tourists flock here to see me calving into the sea.

Where am I?

Southeast Trivia

Famous naturalist John Muir quipped on a trip here, "It is raining, however; but the rain is of good quality."

How true! The Southeast holds the record for wet weather, but it also boasts some other less soggy records. See if you can answer these.

?

Clue: I am the largest national forest in America with over 17 million acres. Set aside in 1907 by Teddy Roosevelt, I protect one of the two most northern wintering areas for the Trumpeter Swan.

What am I?

?

Clue: Massachusetts, Rhode Island, and Connecticut could fit within my borders. I have glaciers 5 times the size of Manhattan, and 9 of the 16 highest peaks in North America. There are so many peaks within my boundaries that no one has bothered to name them all.

What am I?

Answer	Answer	Answer	Answer
Chilkat Bald Eagle Preserve	Wrangell - St. Elias National Park & Preserve	Tongass National Forest	Glacier Bay National Park & Preserve

Galloping Glaciers

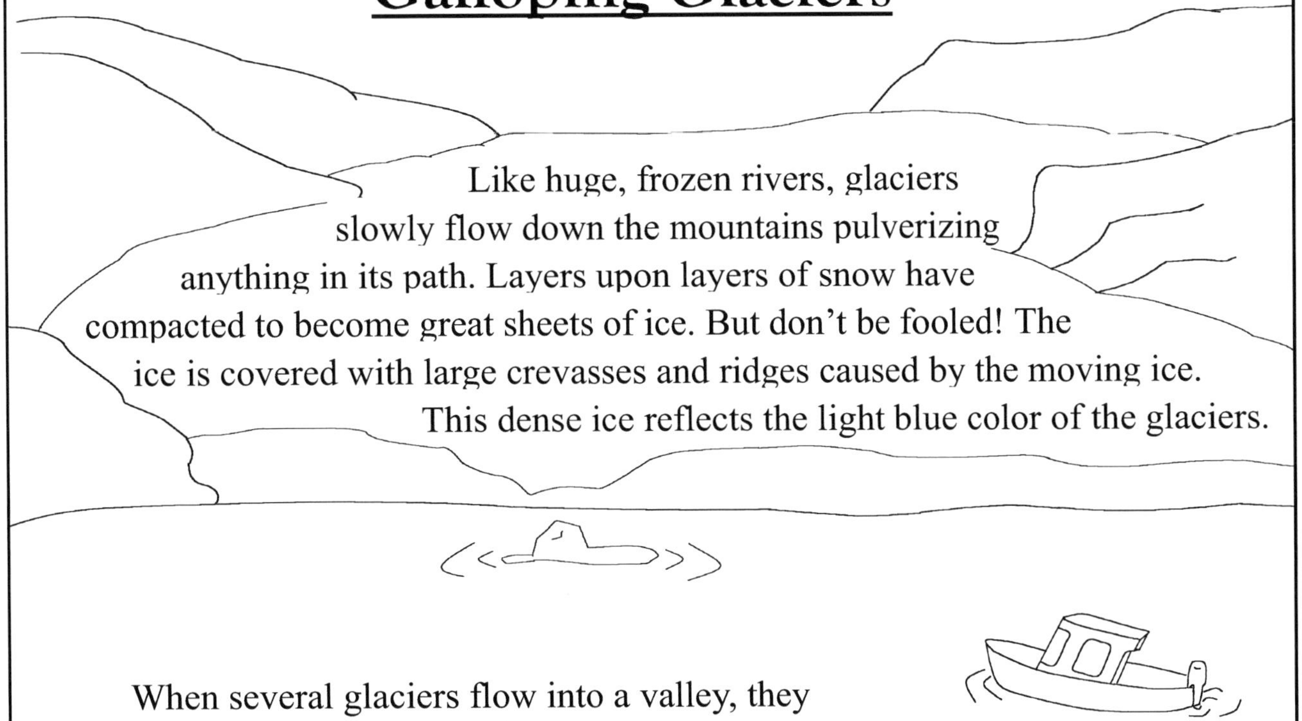

Like huge, frozen rivers, glaciers slowly flow down the mountains pulverizing anything in its path. Layers upon layers of snow have compacted to become great sheets of ice. But don't be fooled! The ice is covered with large crevasses and ridges caused by the moving ice. This dense ice reflects the light blue color of the glaciers.

When several glaciers flow into a valley, they form an *ice field.* Glaciers which terminate or end at the salt water are called tidewater glaciers. These are the type found in Glacier Bay National Park and Preserve. Glaciers *calve* when big chunks of ice break off and fall into the water as *icebergs*.

Incredibly, in the ice, one small creature survives. Do you know what it is?

Color in the areas with the dots to find out.

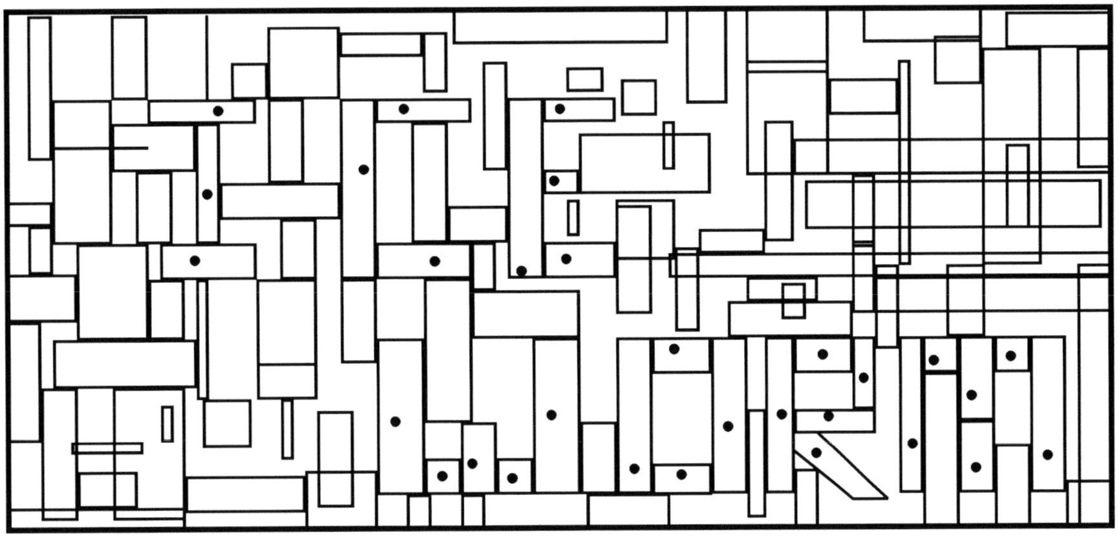

Haidi and Tsimpshian

Southeastern Indians prospered from the thriving salmon and seals in the seas and the moose, deer, and bear on the mountains. With food so abundant they had time to build elaborate homes. They were like fortresses - housing up to 12 families - and decorated with intricate designs or totem poles which told a story or designated a particular clan within the tribe. They also carved canoes from yellow cedar trees. Some of these "canoes" were 75 feet long and could hold 50 men! Not your typical canoe.

The Tsimpshian Indians live only on Annette Island. Their ancestors were brought from British Colombia in 1887 by missionary William Duncan.

The Haidi were known for especially fine totem poles. They settled Alaska's Queen Charlotte Islands hundreds of years ago.

Draw a Totem Pole showing all your favorite animals.

Tlingit

The Tlingits occupied almost all the land of Southeast Alaska. Their society was highly organized between two main clans, the Eagles and the Ravens. The sons of one clan were required to marry only daughters of the other. The clan your mother belonged to determined which clan you belonged to. Each clan was further divided into smaller groups like the Killer Whales, Wolves or Frogs. Each clan had clearly defined responsibilities. If someone died, the other clan would plan the burial. Then the clan of the deceased would host a feast, called a potlatch, as a way to say thank-you. This tradition is similar to those of the Indians all along Washington and Oregon coast, suggesting a common ancestry.

The Tlingits were feared as powerful warriors. The Aleuts refused to travel into Tlingit territory to collect furs for the Russians. To prepare for war, the Tlingits wore painted wooden helmets and breastplates. They fought with spears and long curved knives. They carved and wore elaborate masks of killer whales and bears to intimidate the enemy.

Circle the differences between these two masks. So far we've found 14. How many can you find?

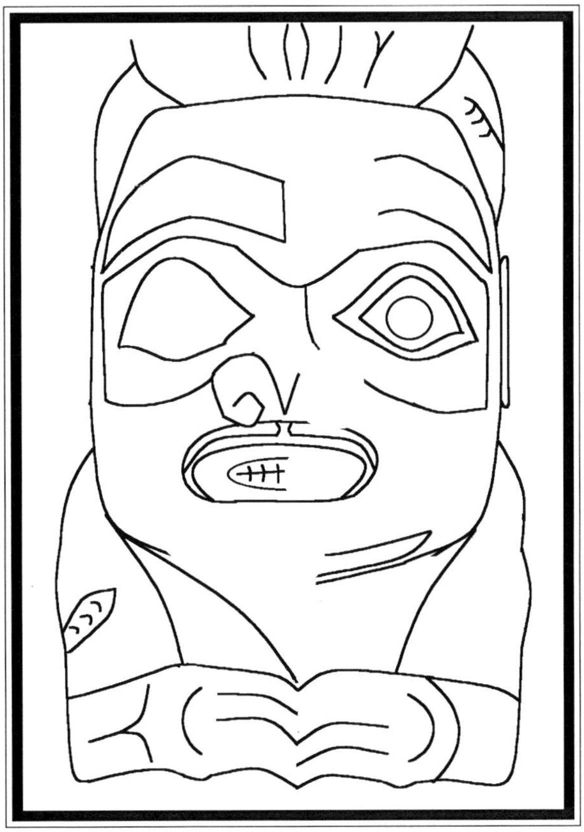

Alaska Close - Up: South-Central Alaska

This region follows the Gulf Coast of Alaska from the Panhandle to the Aleutian Chain and extends north to the border of Denali National Park. Spectacular mountain ranges flank the region, protecting it from the cold, north winds and creating a relatively mild climate. Over 54% of Alaskans live in this area. So the next time someone from the 'lower-48' asks you if everyone in Alaska lives in igloos, just smile and invite them for a ride on your dogsled.

How well do you know the cities of South - Central? Answer the clues using the names below and complete the puzzle.

Soldotna
Homer
Kenai
Wasilla
Cordova
Seldovia
Palmer
Seward
Valdez
Anchorage

Across

1. With a spit extending into Kachemak Bay, ___ ___ ___ ___ ___ really is "the end of the road" - or at least the end of the Sterling Highway.

2. ___ ___ ___ ___ ___ ___ ___ ___ ___ is the headquarters of two of Alaska's largest military bases.

3. The original town of ___ ___ ___ ___ ___ ___ was destroyed in the 1964 Good Friday Earthquake.

4. The town of ___ ___ ___ ___ ___ ___ ___ grew as a shipping port for the Kennecott Copper Mine.

5. ___ ___ ___ ___ ___ ___ ___ is the real starting place for the Iditarod Sled Dog Race.

Down

1. ___ ___ ___ ___ ___ ___ is the location of the only musk ox domestication project in the world.

2. ___ ___ ___ ___ ___ ___ ___ ___ was originally the largest city on the lower Kenai Peninsula.

3. The Alaska Railroad's southern terminus (or end) is in ___ ___ ___ ___ ___ ___.

4. ___ ___ ___ ___ ___ began as a fish camp for the Athabaskan Indians at the mouth of the Kenai River.

5. ___ ___ ___ ___ ___ ___ ___ ___ is the major population center of the Kenai Peninsula.

Matanuska Valley

In 1929 the Great Depression hit the United States. Many people lost their jobs. Many farmers lost their farms.

To help the farmers, the government settled 200 farmers and their families in the rich Matanuska Valley to farm. They became known as the Matanuska Valley Colony. Their descendants continue to farm the land which has since become the "breadbasket of Alaska." They also started a dairy, "Matanuska Maid," which continues to supply milk and dairy products all over Alaska.

Moving Mountains: Earthquakes and Volcanoes

Many of the spectacular mountain ranges in South-Central Alaska and all along the southern coast exist because of the moving ground under our feet. Alaska borders the Pacific Plate - a massive slab of the earth's crust under the Pacific Ocean which tends to shift north on the molten rock bubbling underneath.

The movement of the Pacific Plate builds up pressure, like soda pop in a can. When the pressure builds too high, a volcano blows its top or an earthquake rattles the mountains. The largest earthquake in North America occurred in Alaska on Good Friday in 1964. Estimated at 9.2 on the Richter scale, it and the *tsunami* (tidal wave) it triggered, destroyed entire towns on the coast like Seward and Valdez and did untold damage throughout the South-Central Region.

Alaska has more than 70 active or potentially active volcanoes. While most are far from the population centers, three on the west side of Cook Inlet have erupted within the last twenty years. The latest erupted in 1992. Do you know which one it was?

Solve the riddle to find out the most recent eruption in Alaska.

With birds on my left and a path down the mountain, I have the sound of a contented cat in my name.

Which one am I?

Mt. Redoubt

Mt. Spurr

Mt. Augustine

Alaska Close - Up: Interior Region

The Interior Region covers over a third of the state, an area about the size of Colorado. To the south is Mt. McKinley. At 20,300 feet it is the highest peak in North America. To the north, lying above the Artic Circle, the Brooks Range serves as a natural boundary between the Interior and the North Slope Region. Slicing across the Interior, the mighty Yukon River cuts a path southwest for 1,875 miles.

Winters are dark and cold. Temperatures average from zero to –20 degrees Fahrenheit. Summers are typically sunny and warm with temperatures in the 70's and higher.

Alaska's second largest city, Fairbanks, began as a trading center during the gold rush. Known as the "Golden Heart of Alaska," it now serves as a transportation and staging area for Prudhoe Bay and the outlying villages.

Kiska is touring the Interior. Follow his stops below to find out where he is now.

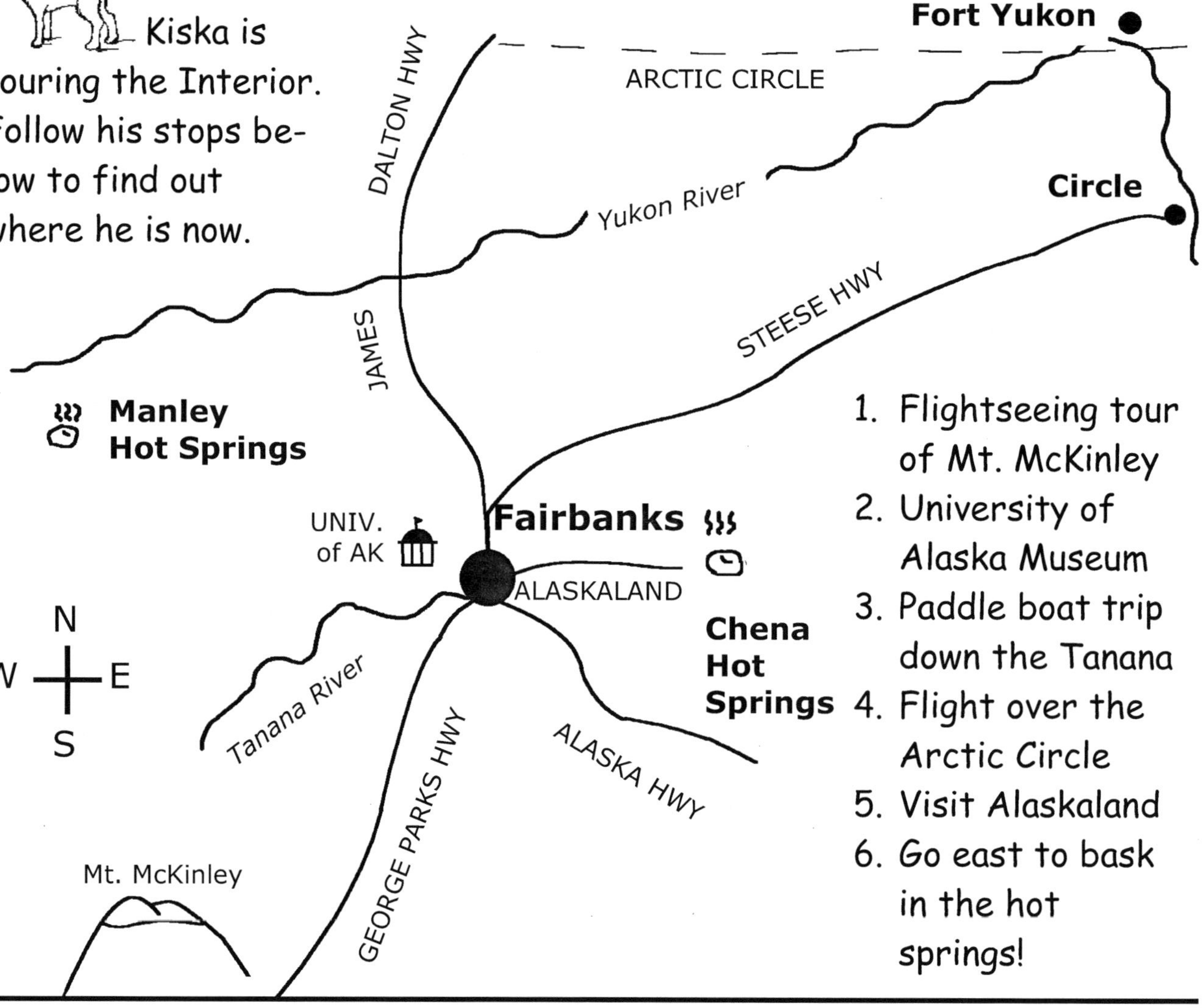

1. Flightseeing tour of Mt. McKinley
2. University of Alaska Museum
3. Paddle boat trip down the Tanana
4. Flight over the Arctic Circle
5. Visit Alaskaland
6. Go east to bask in the hot springs!

Athabascans

The Athabascans were hunting and fishing tribes who lived along the rivers of the Interior and traveled with the herds. They were also the original inhabitants of much of the South-Central Region. They developed snowshoes to track their game in winter. They were such skilled hunters, many became contract trappers for the Russians and Americans. Today, they are known for their elaborate beadwork.

Athabascans are believed to be related to the Navajos and Apaches of the American Southwest. They share many of the same native words.

Athabascans referred to Mt. McKinley as Denali or "The Great One." They were drawn to its slopes for the grizzlies, caribou, moose, and Dall sheep which migrate throughout the area.

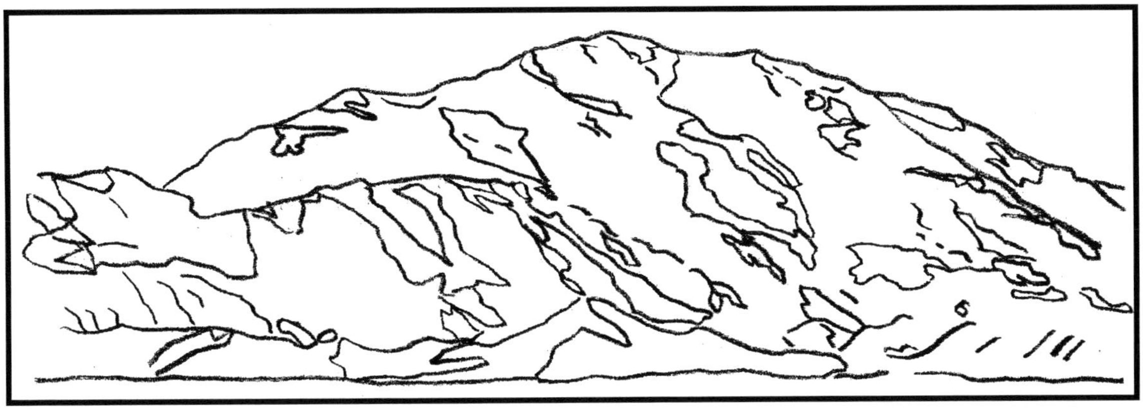

Do you know what the name Athabascan means? Use the secret code to find out.

" ___ ___ ___ ___ ___   ___ ___ ___ ___   ___ ___ ___
7 18 1 19 19   8 5 18 5   1 14 4

___ ___ ___ ___ ___ "
20 8 5 18 5

Secret Code

A	B	C	D	E	F	G	H	I	J	K	L	M	N	O	P	Q	R	S	T	U	V	W	X	Y	Z
1	2	3	4	5	6	7	8	9	10	11	12	13	14	15	16	17	18	19	20	21	22	23	24	25	26

Alaska Close - Up: North Slope Region

The only road to "the Slope" (as most Alaskans call this area) is the Dalton Highway from Fairbanks to Prudhoe Bay. To reach Barrow, Kotzebue, or any of the smaller villages or national parks like the Gates of the Artic, you will have to fly.

This arctic area is mostly a treeless tundra. In the summer over 100 kinds of birds and 440 varieties of small plants and wildflowers fill the tundra. The average temperature is 40 degrees in the summer and –17 degrees in the winter. Temperatures can spike, however, to 80 degrees Fahrenheit in the summer and fall to –80 degrees in winter. Brrr! (That's an understatement!)

This region is best known for its black gold - oil! The richest oil strike in North America was made at Prudhoe Bay. The original lease sale in 1969 brought $900 million into the state's coffers. The Trans-Alaska Pipeline was built in 1977 to carry oil from Prudhoe Bay over 800 miles south to the ice-free port of Valdez.

What is the northernmost point on the North American continent?

___ ___ ___ ___ ___ ___
1 2 3 4 5 6

Answer these questions, then fill in the spaces with the letters in the boxes to find out. Here's a list of words to choose from: jade, arctic, two, polar, summer, barrels.

1. Enough [ ] ___ ___ ___ ___ ___ ___ of oil were sold in the first shipment to equal the original purchase price of Alaska—$7.2 million.

2. Eskimo's make jewelry from ___ [ ] ___ ___, the state gem.

3. The largest active sand dunes in the ___ [ ] ___ ___ ___ ___ are found at Kobuk National Park.

4. The sun is up here for two months every ___ ___ ___ ___ ___ [ ].

5. The ___ [ ] ___ ___ ___ bear is the largest in Alaska.

6. The sun sets here for ___ [ ] ___ months every winter.

Eskimos

Related to the Mongolian peoples of Siberia, Eskimos settled thousands of years ago all along the north coast and Bering Sea, down to the Aleutian Islands. Relatives still travel between the Russian Far East and Alaska. Big Diomede Island, Russia, and Little Diomede Island, Alaska, are only three miles apart.

Creative and skilled, Eskimos used the natural resources around them to adapt to life in the treeless tundra. Since their main diet consisted of sea animals, like seal, whale, and walrus, they built *umiaks* and *kayaks* to hunt on the ocean. They carved spearheads and *ulus* from ivory to catch and clean their harvest. They made dog sleds with ivory or whalebone runners. They used whalebones and driftwood to build underground houses for the winter. They wore skin parkas and *mukluks* from seal, bear, or marmot, and made raincoats from animal intestines. To block the glare from the sun on water or snow, they fashioned sunglasses from bone or wood with slits to see through.

Eskimos consist of two main groups today. The Inupiat live in the far north. The Yup'ik live in the Yukon-Kuskokwim Delta along the southwest coast. These are the largest of Alaska's native groups.

How well do you know your Eskimo? Try to guess what these words mean by matching the Eskimo word to its correct definition.

1. Umiak	A. Polar bear
2. Ulu	B. Raw whale blubber
3. Inuk	C. Means "Real People"
4. Akutaq	D. Eskimo ice cream
5. Apa	E. Large boat
6. Atigi	F. Parka
7. Maktaq	G. Means "Man"
8. Yup'ik	H. Grandfather
9. Nanuq	I. Woman's Knife

Alaska Close - Up: Bering Sea Coast

The Bering Sea Coast Region extends from the Arctic Circle down to the Aleutian Mountain Range. Let's start in the north. The first town you would come to is Nome on the Seward Peninsula. If you came in the late 1800's, you (and 20,000 other people) could have picked up gold off the beach.

Continuing on, you would follow the Norton Sound down to the Yukon-Kuskokwim Delta. The massive Yukon and Kuskokwim Rivers meander through this lowland to the Bering Sea. The area is home to more than a million ducks, geese, swans, and other birds in the Yukon Delta National Wildlife Refuge. Bethel is the hub community for the area.

Farther south are the rich fishing grounds of Bristol Bay. Ships dock at Dillingham to provide supplies for the smaller villages. You could buy any kind of small animal furs from weasels, beavers, lynx, muskrat, and fox from the natives who trap and sell them. Now you've reached the Alaska Peninsula and the end of your journey, at least this one.

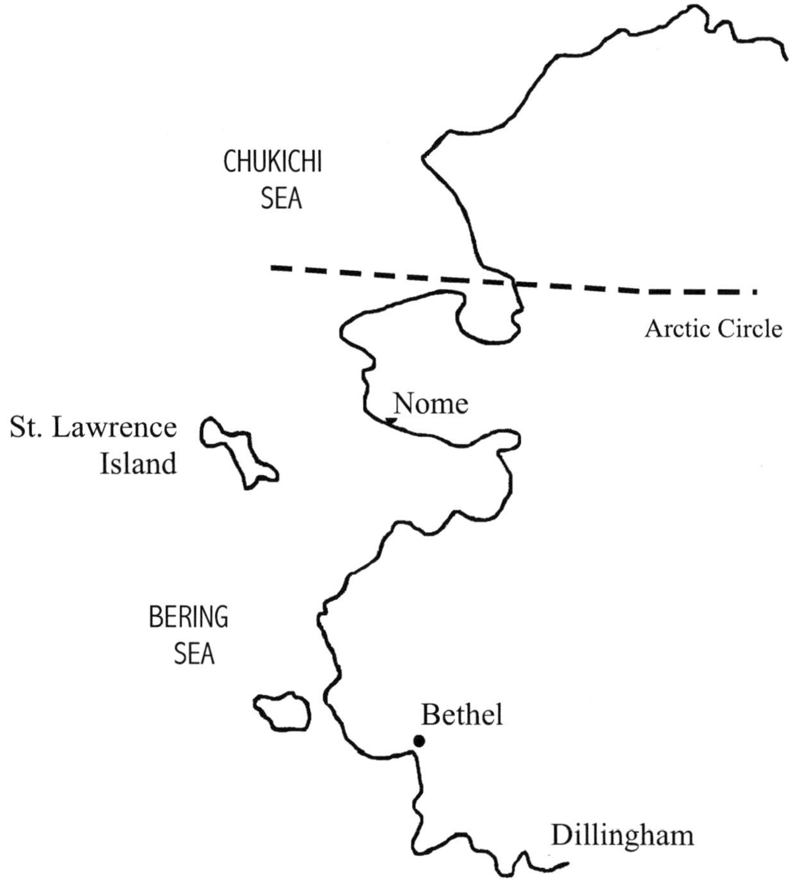

It's Doodle Time! What does this sea coast look like to you? Draw it in.

Iditarod

Nome is the finish line for the "Last Great Race." What used to be a dog team mail route is now the trail for the annual dog-sled race known as the Iditarod. Every year on the first Saturday in March, mushers leave Anchorage for the ceremonial start of the race. (The real start is in Wasilla.) Upwards to fifteen dogs and a musher fight mountain passes, frozen bogs, windswept rivers to get to Nome. The grueling trip usually takes ten to twenty-one days. Mushers and their dogs fly in from around the world to compete in this unique sport.

Mushers have their own unique language with their dogs. See if you know the following commands. Here are the words you can choose from:

Hike! Whoa! Haw! Gee! Easy! Trail! Come Gee! Come Haw!

Start the team: ________

Turn left: ________

Turn right: ________

Turn right 180 degrees: ________

Turn left 180 degrees: ________

Slow down: ________

Request for trail right-of-way: ________

Stop: ________

Alaska Close - Up: Aleutian Chain

At the head of the Aleutian Chain is the Alaska Peninsula which extends about 550 miles into the Pacific Ocean. A chain of islands follows, sweeping 1,200 miles into the sea. The land is mountainous, but generally treeless and windy.

Katmai National Park on the Alaska Peninsula attests to more recent volcanic activity. In 1912, a huge volcanic eruption sent lava spilling into the valley below. Smoke and gases created thousands of holes (called *fumaroles*) as they escaped through the hot lava. Hence the name of the valley became "Valley of 10,000 Smokes." The steam lasted for 20 years, and the ash from the explosion colored the sky around the world. Many volcanoes in the region continue to be active.

Fish and wildlife flourish in the area. Kodiak, Cold Bay, and Dutch Harbor are centers for fishing and crabbing. Kodiak is known for its Alaskan Brown Bear which can weigh in at a whopping 1,200 lbs.

It's WAR!

Fill in this picture to see the Zero, the dreaded Japanese bomber.

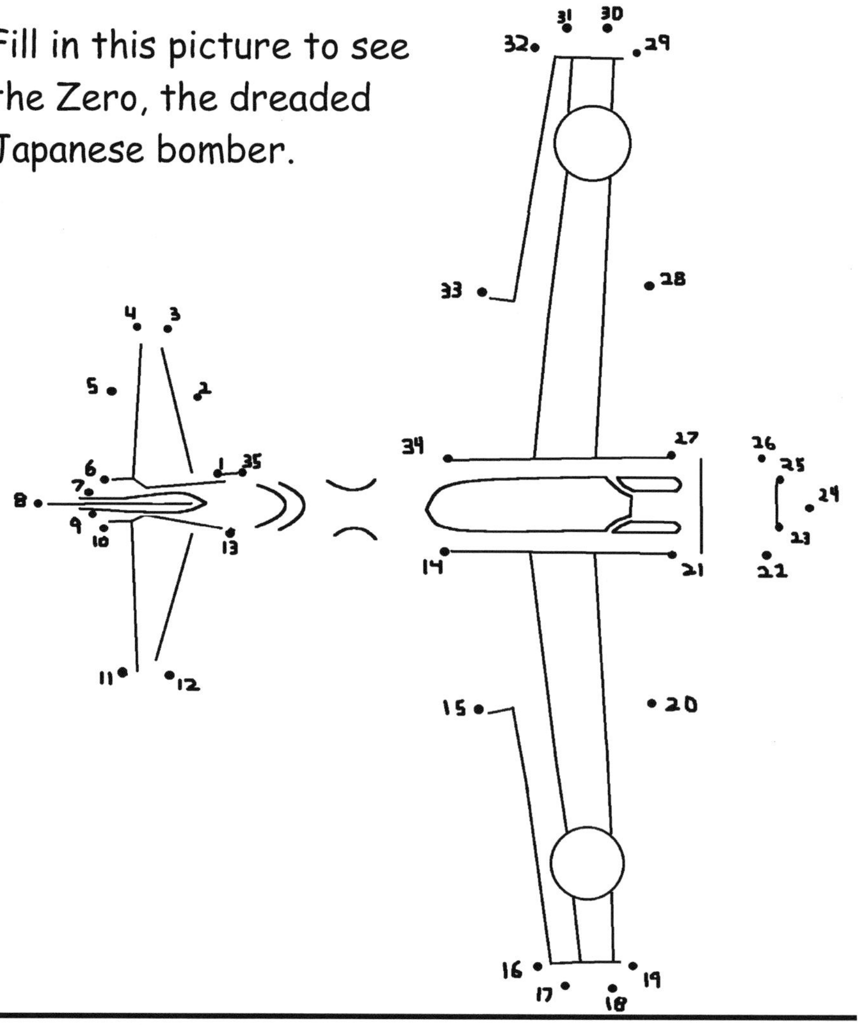

Did you know?

On December 7, 1941 Japan bombed Pearl Harbor in an ambitious plan to control the Pacific. Six months later, they bombed Dutch Harbor and invaded Kiska and Attua, the farthest islands of the Aleutian Chain. These islands were was the only occupied U.S. territory during World War II. It took fourteen months and two major, costly battles to retake the islands.

Aleuts

It is from the Aleuts that we get the name of our state. They referred to the land east of their home as "al-ay-ek-sha" or the Great Land.

Similar to the Eskimos, but with a different language, the Aleuts lived off the abundance of the sea. They built skin-covered kayaks called *baidarkas* to hunt sea otter, sea lion, or seal. They not only ate the animals, but used the soft skins for clothes, the intestines for waterproof parkas, the flippers for the soles of their boots, and the oil for lamps. They also carved excellent arrowheads and fishhooks from bones. The women wove intricately designed grass baskets.

To escape the rain, fog and wind, the Aleuts built homes, half buried, with driftwood and sod. The door was in the ceiling to keep out the wind. They climbed down notched logs to get in. About 10 families lived together separated by grass mat walls.

Russian explorers enslaved the Aleuts to hunt for otter. Later the American government relocated the Aleuts to the Southeast when the Japanese invaded during World War II. Many died in the unfamiliar environment. After the war, they returned to their homes.

Aleuts were excellent hunters. They even used a special tool to catch a bird in flight. Write the first letter of the names of the animals or object below to find out what it was.

____ ____ ____ ____

Definition: Four to six strings knotted together at one end with small rocks tied to the other. Thrown at birds flying overhead to entangle one and bring it down.

Alaska In History: Outline of Alaska History

The following pages list many important events in Alaska's history along with some of Alaska's most interesting people. At the end are three History Quizzes for you to try. But remember — this is not a textbook. Go ahead and doodle on the pictures or add other dates you think are important!

Prehistoric - 1600's

Long ago Alaska was a very different place. Lush, green and wet - like a tropical rain forest - large animals with big appetites lived here. Dinosaurs, woolly mammoths, sloths, lions, and saber-toothed tigers roamed the slopes with moose, antelope, and camels.

When the weather turned cold and the Ice Age began many of these animals died. Some were frozen intact like "Blue Babe," a mummified steppe bison. (You can visit him at the University of Alaska Museum in Fairbanks.) Fossils have been found all over the state. There are even dinosaur tracks in Barrow! All that lush greenery they fed on became the oil we use now.

Eventually, the ice began to melt and wild game began to return to the forests and plains. Hunters followed the animals. Scientists believe some of these hunters crossed and ancient land bridge over what is now the Bering Sea. Others came from Canada.

These peoples were the great, great, great, great, great–grandparents of the Alaska natives of today. The Athabaskans followed the fish up the rivers into the Interior of Alaska. Eskimos and Aleuts hunted along the northern and western coasts. The Tlingits and Haida settled along the lush southeastern coast.

They were virtually undisturbed by outsiders for thousands of years until Peter the Great of Russia began to wonder if Russian and North America were connected.

1700's

1724 Czar of Russia, Peter the Great, sends Vitus Bering (a Danish man serving in the Russian navy) on an expedition to the Russian Far East and America's north coast.

Vitus Bering
(What would he look like with glasses?)

1727 Vitus Bering and his crew finally reach Russia's coast after trekking across the freezing cold and steep mountains of Siberia for a year and a half.

1728 Bering builds a ship, the *Saint Gabriel*, and sails for America where he and his crew sight St. Lawrence Island, but fog and ice force them to return to Russia.

1741 Bering and Aleksey Chirikov, a Russian explorer, set off in two ships, the *Saint Peter* and the *Saint Paul*, to try to reach America. Chirikov in the *Saint Paul* spots Southeast Alaska, but bad weather and lack of food force them to return to Russia.

Bering and his crew wander in the fog until finally on July 16, the fog lifts and the towering peaks of the Saint Elias Mountain Range appear before them. They anchor on what is now Kayak Island - the first Europeans ever recorded to set foot on Alaskan soil!

Old Tlingit Legend

Though Chirikov never made it ashore, he did send two boatloads of men out to try to find food and supplies. The men were never seen again. However, there is an old Tlingit tale that describes how a crafty Tlingit warrior, dressed in a bear skin, lured a group of white men into an ambush. Does this describe the fate of Chirikov's men? We don't know for sure.

1700's

1742 Caught in a violent storm and desperately weakened by scurvy (a disease caused by a lack of Vitamin C), Bering's ship wrecks on an island off Russia. Bering and many sailors die. Surviving the winter on sea otter, the other sailors rebuild the ship and return to Russian with a vast wealth in sea otter pelts.

1743 Sea otter pelts change Alaska history. Russian traders begin to aggressively hunt Alaskan sea otters, often enslaving the expert Aleut hunters, so that by the end of the 1700's only 2,000 Aleuts remained of a total estimated population of 25,000.

1763 First European contact with the natives on Kodiak (a mispronunciation of the Inuit name "Kadiak," which means "island.")

1768 Russians establish a trading port in Unalaska.

1775 Attracted by rumors of abundant furs, Spain sends ships up the coast from Mexico. Landing near Sitka, Captain Jaun Francisco dela Bodega y Quadra claims Alaska's southern coast for Spain. (That is why Alaska has towns with Spanish names like Valdez and Cordova.)

1778 British Captain James Cook explores Alaska to the Bering Straight.

1784 Russians build their first permanent settlement, Three Saints Bay, Kodiak.

How Anchor Point Got Its Name

Sailing into the inlet that bears his name, Captain Cook lost a kedge anchor in the intense tidal current. Subsequently, he called the area Anchor Point.

1700's

1789 Spain captures the British fort at Nootka Sound.

1791 Russians build Fort Saint Nicholas on the site of an ancient Athabascan Indian village. Calling the natives "Kenitze," the site becomes known as Kenai.

1792 Spain relinquishes its rights to Alaska after losing the battle over the British fort.

1793 George Vancouver charts the Pacific Coast to Cook Inlet, naming such areas as Prince William Sound, Cape of Prince of Whales, and Bristol Bay. Explorers rely on his charts for over a century.

1794 First Russian Orthodox missionaries arrive in Alaska.

1799 Aleksandr Baranov moves the headquarters of the Russian America Company from Kodiak to Sitka.

BIOGRAPHY: Aleksandr Baranov

(Give this poor fellow a hat!)

Aleksandr Baranov, son of a Russian shop-keeper, arrived on Kodiak in 1791 as the manager for the Russia American Company. A short, balding, and physically unimpressive man, he nevertheless carved an empire out of the Alaskan wilderness over the next 27 years, earning himself the title "Lord of Alaska."

He established his capital at Fort Saint Michael, called "Shee Atika" by the Tlingits. He had to retake the site after Tlingits burned the fort in 1802. He rebuilt the town naming it "New Archangel," though most referred to it as Sitka.

Under the 13 governors who followed Baranov, Sitka became known as the "Paris of the Pacific." It flourished with fine dining, fancy halls and theatre productions - all this while San Francisco was just a mission outpost!

1800's

1802 Tlingits destroy the Russian fort at Sitka.

1804 Baranov attacks the Tlingits with a Russian war ship and rebuilds Sitka, calling it "New Archangel."

1805 New Archangel becomes the capital of Russian America, and Baranov becomes its first governor.

1818 Lt. Otto Von Kotzebu "discovers" the ancient trading center "Kikiktagruk" and claims it for Russia, calling it Kotzebue.

Russians build Alexandrovski Redoubt (or fort); it eventually is renamed Dillingham after US Senator Paul Dillingham.

1824 Father Ivan Veniaminov, a Russian Orthodox missionary, arrives in Unalaska.

<u>BIOGRAPHY: Father Ivan Veniaminov</u> Russian Orthodox missionaries have left a lasting influence on communities all over Alaska. Perhaps none was more indomitable than Father Ivan Veniaminov who first arrived with his family in Unalaska in 1824. He learned the Aleut language, created an alphabet, taught the natives to read, and translated the gospels. He also instructed them in carpentry, blacksmithing, and brickmaking. For ten years he served throughout the Aleutian Islands, traveling as much as 14 – 16 hours a day in a kayak for 4 months every summer to reach the outlying villages.

Such zeal crippled his feet so he moved to Sitka. While there, he built Saint Michael's Cathedral.

In 1868, Father Veniaminov became the Metropolitan of Moscow, the highest ranking position in the Russian Orthodox Church.

1800's

1840 The British Hudson's Bay Company leases Fort Stikine from Russia. (Today known as Wrangell, this is the only Alaskan town to have served under Russian, British, and American flags.)

1846 Transfiguration of Our Lord Russian Orthodox Church built in Ninilchik.

1847 Hudson's Bay Company builds Fort Yukon.

1867 United States buys Alaska from Russia for $7.2 million in March. Flags switched in a formal ceremony in October at Sitka, the capital.

BIOGRAPHY: William Henry Seward

(This man deserves a badge !)

Secretary of State William Seward is the man known for buying Alaska from Russia. But he almost did not live to make that deal. A staunch abolitionist during the Civil War, he was recovering from a carriage accident when a man named Lewis Powell forced his way into Seward's room. Misfiring his gun, he attacked Seward with a Bowie knife, slashing his face. A male nurse managed to chase Powell away.

At the same time across town, John Wilkes Booth shot Abraham Lincoln. Later, authorities learned Booth and Powell had conspired together to kill both Lincoln and Seward.

Seward went on to negotiate the $7.2 million deal to buy Alaska from Russia. Russia's interest in Alaska lagged with the declining seal populations and their own internal conflict. For less than $.02 an acre, America gained a land rich in gold, copper, oil, and other natural resources. At the time, however, most only thought of Alaska as a big ice cube and called the deal "Seward's Folly."

1800's

1869 Seldovia (from the Russian word "Seldevoy" meaning "herring bay") established as a trading post.

1877 Dr. Sheldon Jackson first arrives in Alaska.

BIOGRAPHY: Dr. Sheldon Jackson At a time when Alaska was a vast unknown to most Amercians, Presbyterian minister Dr. Sheldon Jackson visited the new territory. Zealous in his beliefs and impassioned by the need he saw, he became Alaska's most vocal lobbyist for the next 30 years.

Proclaiming Alaska's need from the west coast to Washington D.C., he inspired a public outcry from Presbyterians, Baptists, Methodists, Episcopalians, and the National Education Association. The result was the Organic Act of Alaska which brought some law and order to the wilderness by placing the territory under the laws of Oregon and providing a judge and other civil officials, as well as appropriating $25,000 for education.

Sheldon Jackson was named Alaska's educational administrator. By 1888, Alaska had 16 staffed schools. He also founded the college that bears his name in Sitka.

Jackson was also the reason for reindeer in Alaska. Concerned for starving Eskimos in the Aleutians, he lobbied congress for money to bring a reindeer herd from Siberia. Although these died from the wet weather, an undaunted Jackson lobbied for another herd, and this time sent them farther north where they flourished.

1880 Chief Kowee leads Joe Juneau and Richard Harris to Gold Creek, and Juneau, the first Alaska gold rush town, is born! Douglas and Treadwell also spring up as gold rush towns around the Gastineau Channel.

1881 Chilkat Indians allow Presbyterian Minister S. Young Hall to build a mission and school at Haines or "Dtehshuh" meaning "end of the trail."

1800's

1881 US Army establishes a meteorological research center in Barrow. (The Eskimos called it "Ukpeagvik" - or "place where owls hunt." The British named it Barrow after Sir John Barrow, 2nd Secretary of the British Admiralty.)

BIOGRAPHY: Joe Juneau

(Give Joe the gold!)

"We struck it rich!" Joe Juneau was a penniless gold seeker in 1880 when Chief Kowee lead Juneau and his partner Richard Harris to Gold Creek. They staked a 160 acre claim beside the Gastineau Channel and the first Alaskan gold rush town was born! The Juneau mine (A-J or Alaska-Juneau Mine) produced over $80 million dollars in gold until it closed in 1944. Juneau prospered, nonetheless, as Alaska's capital.

Juneau and Harris did not fair so well. Harris spent all $75,000 in gold he found and died broke in an Oregon sanitarium. Juneau went through all his $18,000 and died in Dawson city in 1899 searching for more gold. Fellow miners honored his wish and raised $400 to ship his body back to the town they named for him.

1884 Organic Act passes extending the laws of the state of Oregon to Alaska and creating a court system to bring justice to the lawless North.

This same year the Moravian Church establishes a mission at Bethel or "Mumtrekhlogamute" meaning "smokehouse people" in Yupik.

1885 Mike Martin buys 160 acres from Chief Kyan to build what is known today as Ketchikan. Tlingits used the area along the "Kitschk-hin" creek as a fish camp; the name meant "thundering wings of an eagle."

1887 Anglican Minister William Duncan brings Tsimshian Indians from Canada to settle on Annette Island, Alaska.

1800's

1890 Norwegian Peter Bushmann begins a cannery using clean ice from the nearby glacier; this becomes Petersburg Industries in Petersburg or "Little Norway."

1896 Homer Pennock arrives on the spit in the town later named for him, Homer.

Prospectors discover gold in Klondike, Canada, and the rush is on! Skagway, door to the Klondike, booms to a population of 20,000.

BIOGRAPHY: Soapy Smith Jefferson Randolph Smith arrived in Skagway in October 1897 with five cronies. From a respected Southern family, he began as a swindler by selling marked bars of soap containing $20 or $50 dollar bills to his pals. Unsuspecting passerbys would purchase a bar for $5 to get in on the game, but wind up with nothing except an expensive bar of soap. Hence, he earned his nickname "Soapy."

(What would you pay to bring this crook in?)

Soapy immediately saw his chance in Skagway as thousands of naive and ignorant cheechakos swarmed in looking to strike it rich in the Klondike goldfields. He and his henchmen built a criminal empire of pickpocketers, muggers, and swindling schemes of every kind. He even set up a fake telegraph office, offering to send and receive telegraph messages for $5 each way. (Alaska did not have a telegraph line until 1903.) He wrote the fake replies.

Eventually his schemes caught up with him. An outside judge was called in. When guards were sent to arrest him, Soapy rushed onto the wharf, stopping directly in front of one of the guards. They pulled their guns and shot point blank. Soapy dropped dead. The guard died 12 days later.

1897 Prospector George Crowe, trailing a wounded moose near Circle, finds an unusually warm spring. Following it to its source he discovers Circle Hot Springs.

Gold is discovered at Willow Creek; the town of Willow is established.

1800's

1898 Alaska's first railroad built connecting Skagway to Whitehorse and Anvil Gold Mines in Canada.

1899 Gold discovered laying on the beaches in Nome!

1900's

1900 Judge James Wickersham arrives in the gold rush town of Eagle.

BIOGRAPHY: Judge James Wickersham

Judge James Wickersham originally came to Alaska as a judge for Eagle in 1900. Establishing a reputation as tough and honest, he was called to Nome in 1901 to replace Judge Arthur Noyes who with Alexander Mckenzie, a powerful Republican lobbyist, almost swindled several multi-million dollar claims from their legitimate owners.

After restoring order in Nome, he served throughout several Alaskan towns. In 1908 he became the Alaskan delegate to congress. He worked tirelessly to achieve Alaskan home-rule until finally President Taft signed Wickersham's home-rule bill, the Organic Act of 1912 on August 24. It was Wickersham's 55th birthday.

1901 Captain E.T. Barnett establishes a trading post on the Chena River.

1902 Felix Pedro discovers gold near Barnett's trading post. Barnett's post grows as the Chena steamboat brings loads of prospectors to the area. Later the town is named Fairbanks after Senator Charles Fairbanks who became vice-president.

1903 Judge Wickersham moves the judicial headquarters from Eagle to Fairbanks.

Jim Duke establishes a trading post at "Toghotthele" or "mountain that parallels the river," known today as Nenana.

1900's

1903 Lt. Billy Mitchell completes the first Alaskan telegraph line connecting Russia to New York, opening Alaska to civilization.

1906 Alaska moves its capital from Sitka to Juneau.

1908 Kennecott Copper Mine established. The richest concentration of copper ore in the world, it produced $200 million in ore.

1912 Organic Act establishes home-rule for Alaska.

1913 First air flight in Alaska.

1914 Tent city erected on the banks of Ship Creek as workers arrive to work on the construction of the railroad from Seward to Fairbanks. Subsequently a "Great Anchorage Land Sale" sold lots to the land surrounding the creek, and the town of Anchorage was born.

1916 Palmer established as a railway station.

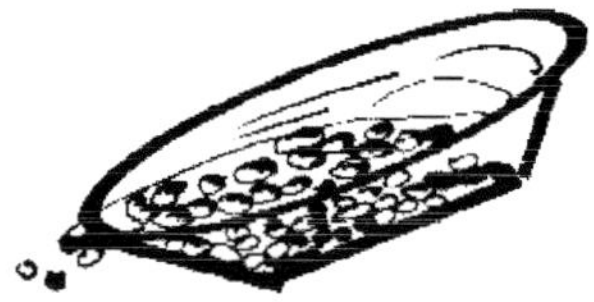

1917 Wasilla developed as a supply base for gold and coal mining. It was named after a respected Indian chief whose name meant "breath of air."

1918 The town of Healy grows up around Usibelli Coal Mine. It continues to be Alaska's largest coal mine, supplying 800,000 tons of coal each year.

1920 Railroad station opens in Talkeetna, an Indian word meaning "where rivers join."

1900's

1923 Alaska Railroad between Anchorage and Fairbanks is completed.

1935 US Government begins the Matanuska Valley Project, relocating 200 farmers from the midwest to Alaska.

1942 Japan bombs Dutch Harbor and invades Attu and Kiska. Working 24 hours a day, seven days a week, US soldiers and civilians build the Al-Can Highway in a record 6 months to bring in military defenses to protect the territory.

1943 After two grim and costly battles, the US drives Japan from Alaska.

1944 Bon Davis homesteads outside Fairbanks, later selling the land to developers who subdivide it and name it North Pole, hoping to attract a toy company.

1947 Constructed as a bridge crossing for the Kenai River, Soldotna grows as a commercial center for the Kenai Peninsula due to its strategic location on the Seward Highway.

1948 US Army builds Whittier as a supply port for World War II; it was named after the American poet John Greenleaf Whittier.

1957 Oil is discovered on the Kenai Peninsula.

1959 Alaska becomes the 49th State!

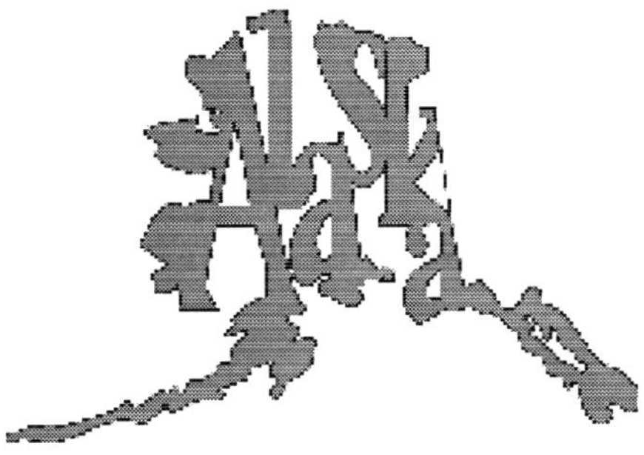

(Can you find all the letters to spell Alaska?)

1900's

1963 The Alaska Marine Highway opens in Southeast Alaska.

1964 Biggest earthquake in North America shakes Alaska.

1968 Huge oil reserves discovered at Prudhoe Bay.

1971 Alaska Native Claims Settlement Act permanently secured 44 million acres of land for the natives and buys other land for $400 million, opening the door for the Trans-Alaska Pipeline.

Iditarod begins as an annual dog sledding race.

1976 Legislature establishes the Permanent Fund - money paid each year to Alaska residents from the interest made from oil revenues.

1977 The first oil flows down the completed Trans-Alaska Pipeline from Prudhoe Bay to Valdez.

1985 Drop in oil prices stifles the Alaskan economy and many go bankrupt.

1988 Vern Tejas makes the first successful winter climb of Mt. McKinley alone.

1989 Exxon Valdez runs aground spilling 11 million gallons of crude oil; massive clean-up ensues.

1991 Bristol Bay fishermen strike over low salmon prices.

1900's

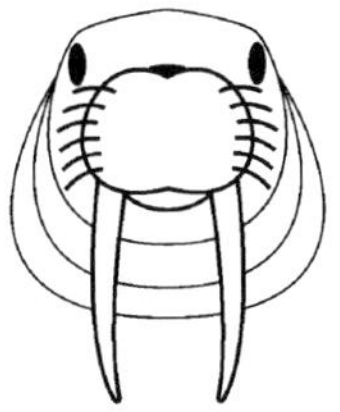

1998 Unemployment at record low - 5.8%.

Seward's Sealife Center opens - the first cold-water marine research facility in the western hemishpere.

1999 Edgar Nollner Sr. passes away. He was the last surviving musher of the 1925 diphtheria serum run to Nome.

Alaska Native Heritage Center opens in Anchorage.

2000's

NORTH TO THE FUTURE!

(Draw yourself!)

This spot is for YOU! YOU are special and have been born at this specific time in history for a purpose. Whether you are a tourist or a resident, Alaska's vast wilderness, unique wildlife, and abundant seas can inspire you to see a future bright with opportunity.

Alaska needs you to become wise scientists, fishermen, doctors, bankers, senators, CEO's, writers, moms, dads, brothers, or sisters to provide leadership for Alaska's future. As tourism and study of Alaska's natural resources grows, the market for seafood becomes more specialized, and the demand for raw materials increases, young men and women of character will have the opportunity to shape this world for the better.

You Kids - from Barrow to Bethel, Homer to Juneau - those leaders are you!

Alaska on the Globe

Where in the world is Alaska?

Prehistoric - 1700's History Quiz

Select your answers from the following words:

sloths	Dinosaur	Prehistoric	sea-otters
1741	Sitka	Cook	Peter
Valdez	Athabaskans	scurvy	1791
Kodiak	Baranov	1793	

1. George Vancouver charts the Pacific Coast in ________________________; explorers use his maps for the next century.

2. At one time, dinosaurs, woolly mammoths, and ________________________ once lived in Alaska.

3. ________________________ was highly civilized with fine dining and fancy balls at a time when San Francisco was just a mission village.

4. Bering and many of his men, weakened by ________________________, died after their ship wreaked in a violent storm.

5. ________________________ became known as "Lord of Alaska."

6. ________________________ lived primarily in the Interior Region of Alaska.

7. Alexsandr Baranov came to Alaska in ________________________ as manager for a Russian trading company.

8. ________________________ is all the history that happened to people and the world before they started writing it down.

9. Bering and his men first landed on Alaskan soil in ________________________.

10. Spain, attracted by the plentiful furs, claimed Alaska's southern coast for her own, and named towns such as ____________________ and Cordova.

11. Russian traders came to Alaska to hunt ____________________ .

12. ________________________ the Great sent Vitus Bering on an expedition to find if Russia and America were connected.

13. Russia built their first permanent settlement on ______________ .

14. ________________________ tracks have been found in Barrow.

15. Captain ____________________ named Anchor Point when he lost an anchor there.

1800's History Quiz

Select your answers from the following words:

Ketchikan	Kotzebue	Barrow	moose
Folly	1880	Tsimpshian	1898
reindeer	1867	Veniaminov	Nome
Soapy	Seward	Wrangell	

1. The swindler ______________________________ Smith set up a fake telegraph office in Skagway during the Klondike Gold Rush.

2. ______________________________ is the only Alaskan town to have served under Russian, British, and American flags.

3. ______________________________ Indians live on Annette Island.

4. Prospectors discover gold lying on the beaches in ______________________________ in 1899!

5. A wounded ______________________________ leads prospector George Crowe to Circle Hot Springs.

6. The first Alaska gold rush town is born when Chief Kowee leads Joe Juneau and his partner to Gold Creek in ______________________________.

7. The ancient trading center "Kikitagruk" was named ______________________________ for the Russian man who "discovered" it.

8. Alaska's first railroad connecting Skagway to Whitehorse is completed in ______________________________.

9. ______________________________ was attacked with a Bowie knife the same night President Lincoln was shot.

10. ____________________________ is called "Ukpeagvik" in Eskimo, meaning "place where owls hunt."

11. Presbyterian minister Dr. Sheldon Jackson introduced ____________________________ to Alaska to help the Eskimos.

12. The United States bought Alaska from Russia for $7.2 million in ____________________________.

13. Secretary of State William Seward negotiated the deal to buy Alaska from Russia - a deal most Americans called "Seward's ____________________________."

14. ____________________________ was the name of the town Mike Martin built on the creek whose Tlingit name meant "thundering wings of an eagle."

15. Russian Orthodox missionary, Father ____________________________, created an alphabet for the Aleuts, translated the Gospels, and taught them to read.

1900's - Present History Quiz

Select your answers from the following words:

Tejas	1959	1925	Attu
You	1957	Kennecott	earthquake
Organic	Fairbanks	Valdez	Anchorage
1963	Black	Wickersham	

1. Oil, called ______________________ Gold, was found in huge amounts at Prudhoe Bay.

2. In ______________________, Alaska became the 49th state!

3. The last surviving musher of the ______________________ diphtheria serum run to Nome dies.

4. The Trans-Alaska Pipeline carries oil from Prudhoe Bay to ______________________.

5. ______________________ was established by Captain Barnett as a trading post, but it grew quickly when Felix Pedro discovered gold nearby.

6. ______________________ are a future leader of Alaska and the world!

7. ______________________ Mine produced over $200 in copper ore.

8. The ______________________ Act of 1912 gave home-rule to Alaska.

9. The Alaska Marine Highway opened in Southeast Alaska in ______________________.

10. Oil was first discovered on the Kenai Peninsula in ______________________________.

11. During World War II, Japan bombed Dutch Harbor and invaded Kiska and ______________________________.

12. Judge ______________________________ restored order in Nome after Judge Noyes and Alexander McKenzie almost successfully swindled several multi-million dollar claims from their rightful owners.

13. Alaska holds the record for the biggest ______________________________ ever recorded in North America.

14. ______________________________ began as a tent city when workers came to work on the railroad.

15. ______________________________ made the first successful climb of Mt. McKinley alone.

Selected Bibliography

Here are some books and websites to learn more about Alaska:

"Community Profiles." Vacation Sites, Inc. 1999. <http://www.vacationalaska.com>.

Ferrell, Nancy Warren. Alaska: A Land in Motion. Fairbanks, AK: University of Alaska, Fairbanks, 1994.

Heinrichs, Ann. Alaska. America the Beautiful. Chicago: Children's Press, 1991.

"Kid's Web Stuff." Alaska State Homepage. 16 Oct. 1999. <http://www.state.ak.us/>.

Niebergall, Jane. The Alaska Report. Homer, AK: Circumpolar Press, 1999.

Wheeler, Keith. The Alaskans. The Old West. Alexandria, VA: Time-Life Books, 1977.

Credits

The Alaska Native Knowledge Network has an excellent site of Alaskan clip art. Check them out!

"Alaska Clipart." Alaska Native Knowledge Network. <http://www.ankn.uaf.edu/clipart.html>.

Index

Answer Key

Page 4

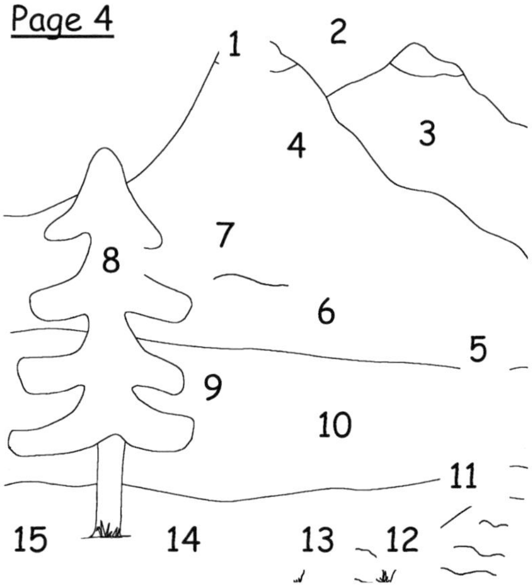

1. Mountain goat
2. Bald Eagle
3. Grizzly Bear
4. Lynx
5. Moose
6. Wolves
7. Caribou
8. Raccoon
9. Red Fox
10. Musk Ox
11. Sandhill Crane
12. Sandpiper
13. Puffin
14. Beaver
15. Porcupine

Page 5

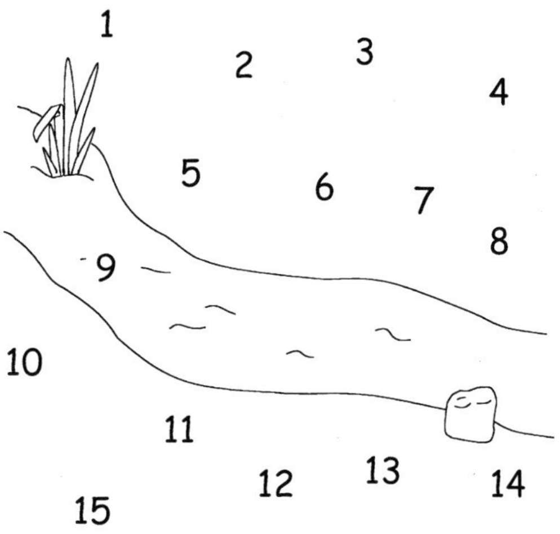

1. Musk Ox
2. Porcupine
3. Mountain Goat
4. Wolf
5. Beaver
6. Lynx
7. Moose
8. Raccoon
9. Sandpiper
10. Red Fox
11. Sandhill Crane
12. Eagle
13. Grizzly Bear
14. Puffin
15. Caribou

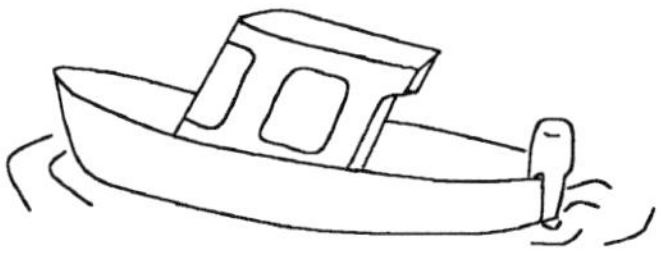

Page 6

.	.	S	.	S	.	C	.	.	O	.	.	.	.	.	.
.	.	N	.	.	E	L	.	.	.	C	.	.	.	.	.
W	H	A	L	E	H	A	L	I	B	U	T	.	.	.	.
.	.	I	.	.	.	M	L	.	.	.	C	O	.	.	.
.	.	L	.	.	S	S	.	.	.	.	.	R	P	.	.
.	.	S	.	.	O	T	.	.	.	.	.	.	A	U	.
.	.	.	T	.	Y	.	A	S	.	.	.	.	.	B	S
.	.	.	R	.	S	.	.	R	K	.	.	.	.	.	H
.	.	.	O	T	T	E	R	.	F	A	.	.	.	.	R
.	.	.	U	.	E	.	.	.	.	I	T	.	.	.	I
.	.	.	T	.	R	.	.	.	.	.	S	E	.	.	M
.	.	.	.	.	S	.	.	.	.	.	A	H	.	.	P
.	.	.	.	.	.	.	.	.	.	.	L	.	.	.	.
.	.	.	.	.	.	.	.	.	.	.	M	.	.	.	.
.	.	.	.	.	.	.	.	.	.	.	O	.	.	.	.
.	.	.	.	.	.	.	.	.	.	.	N	.	.	.	.

Page 7

State Bird: Willow Ptarmigan
State Flower: Forget-me-not

Page 8

State flag: gold stars on a blue background

Page 10

Capital: Juneau
Nickname: Land of the Midnight Sun
Motto: North to the Future
Tree: Sitka Spruce
Mineral: Gold
Gem: Jade
Fish: King Salmon
Sport: Dog Mushing
Fossil: Mastodon
Marine Mammal: Bowhead Whale
Insect: Four-spot Skimmer Dragonfly

Page 10 (continued)

Land Mammal: Moose
Highest Point: Mt. McKinley
Lowest Point: Sea Level
Longest River: Yukon River

Page 11

State Seal:

smelter - mining
ship - sea transportation
trees - wealth in forests
farmer & horse - Alaska's agriculture
fish & seal - importance of fishing and wildlife to Alaska's economy

Page 13

1. Ketchikan
2. Wrangell
3. Petersburg
4. Sitka
5. Juneau
6. Haines
7. Skagway

Page 14

Chilkat Eagle Preserve - Up to 4,000 eagles come to feast here.
Wrangell - St. Elias— Larger than Massachusetts, Rhode Island and Connecticut.
Tongass National Forest- Largest national forest in America.
Glacier Bay- Tourists flock here to see glaciers calving.

Page 15

Ice Worm

Page 17

Page 18

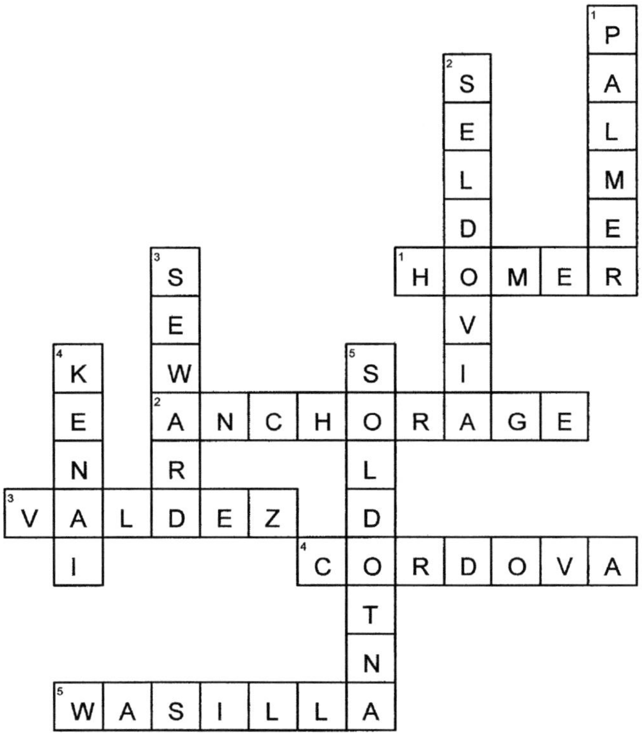

Page 21

Mt. Spurr

Page 22

Chena Hot Springs

Page 23

"Grass Here And There"

Page 24

Barrow - the northernmost point on the North American Continent

1. Barrels
2. Jade
3. Arctic
4. Summer
5. Polar
6. Two

Page 25

1. E.	7. B.
2. I.	8. C.
3. G.	9. A.
4. D.	
5. H.	
6. F.	

Page 27

Start the team: Hike!

Turn left: Haw!

Turn right: Gee!

Turn left 180 degrees: Come Haw!

Turn right 180 degrees: Come Gee!

Request for trail right-of-way: Trail!

Slow down: Easy!

Stop: Whoa!

Page 29

Bola (Bear, Otter, Loon, Alaska)

Pages 45 & 46

1. 1793
2. sloths
3. Sitka
4. scurvy
5. Baranov
6. Athabaskans
7. 1791
8. Prehistoric
9. 1741
10. Valdez
11. Sea otters
12. Peter
13. Kodiak
14. Dinosaur
15. Cook

Pages 47 & 48

1. Soapy
2. Wrangell
3. Tsimshian
4. Nome
5. Moose
6. 1880
7. Kotzebue
8. 1898
9. Seward
10. Barrow
11. Reindeer
12. 1867
13. Folly
14. Ketchikan
15. Veniaminov

Pages 49 & 50

1. Black
2. 1959
3. 1925
4. Valdez
5. Fairbanks
6. You
7. Kennecott
8. Organic
9. 1963
10. 1957
11. Attu
12. Wickersham
13. Earthquake
14. Anchorage
15. Tejas

If you would like to order

additional copies

of Kids' Alaska,

fill out the form on the opposite side and mail to :

Good Roots Press
PO Box 3493
Homer, AK 99603
Email: dave@goodrootspress.com

Or order on the Web at
www.goodrootspress.com

Order Form

1. To order additional copies of this book, complete the following:

_____ Kids' Alaska $12.95 each ________
Qty

+________ Shipping*
________ Total

*Shipping & handling: $3.00 for 1 book; $0.50 for each additional book.
(Contact us for discounts on large orders.)

2. Send Check and Order Form to:

Good Roots Publishing
PO Box 3493
Homer, AK 99603
Email: dave@goodrootspress.com
www.goodrootspress.com

3. Fill in the following (please print):

Name:
Billing Address:
Shipping Address:
City: State: Zip:
Telephone: